WEDDING PARTIES & SHOWERS

*Planning
Memorable
Celebrations*

JO PACKHAM

A Sterling\Chapelle Book
Sterling Publishing Co., Inc. New York

Jo Packham, author

Trice Boerens, illustrator

Tina Annette Brady, designer

Sandra Durbin Chapman, editor

Margaret Shields Marti, editor

Library of Congress Cataloging–in–Publication Data

Packham, Jo.
    Wedding parties & showers : planning memorable celebrations
 / Jo Packham
    p. cm.
    "A Sterling/Chapelle book"
    Includes index
    ISBN 0-8069-8828-2
    1. Showers (Parties) 2. Weddings. I. Title. II. Title: Wedding
parties and showers
GV1472.7.S5P33 1993   92–41335
793.2—dc20   CIP

10 9 8 7 6 5 4 3 2

Published by Sterling Publishing Company, Inc.

387 Park Avenue South, New York, N.Y. 10016

© 1993 by Chapelle Ltd.

Distributed in Canada by Sterling Publishing

C/o Canadian Manda Group, P.O. Box 920, Station U

Toronto, Ontario, Canada M8Z 5P9

Distributed in Great Britain and Europe by Cassell PLC

Villiers House, 41/47 Strand, London WC2N 5JE, England

Distributed in Australia by Capricorn Link Ltd.

P.O.Box 665, Lane Cove, NSW 2066

Manufactured in the United States of America

All Rights Reserved

Sterling ISBN 0-8069-8828-2

Lincoln:

Here is to the friends we meet
and come to know

Contents

Please come
to a
Party

Engagement Party

Getting engaged! For some, it happens suddenly when one night on bended knee he proposes. For others, it may be slower as you grow more confident of each other's love and daily share plans for your future. Or, it might happen with a flair when he has the waiter bring out a handmade pastry aglow with candles and "Will you marry me?" written in chocolate swirls.

Engagement Party

No matter how it happens, getting engaged stirs a whirlwind of emotions that bring daydreams into the realm of reality and sends you spinning into the future. Parties and plans and the delightful feeling of being the bride are what you have to look forward to once the news is out that you are going to be married. After your engagement has been announced, formally or informally, several parties, showers, and dinners are certain to be given in your honor.

The engagement party, the first of such celebrations, traditionally takes place after you have told immediate family and friends of your engagement and upcoming marriage but before the announcement appears in the newspapers. In very large communities, the announcement may come out in the newspaper before the engagement party, or it is becoming common practice to have the engagement party the same day the announcement appears in the paper. There is usually six months to one year from the time of the announcement to the wedding date.

Traditionally, it is the custom to have the engagement party given by the parents of the bride. It is becoming more common to have the party hosted by the parents of the groom-to-be or close friends. If you and the groom are older and have been on your own for a while, you may even want to give the party yourselves.

If yours is a non-traditional family, your choices should be made in consideration of the feelings of those involved–you, your parents and, perhaps, stepparents. Just because there is a divorce in the family, these events need not be awkward.

If your mother or your mother and stepfather are hosting the party, you will want to ask your father to attend and for his guest list. If your father is remarried and his wife is not accepted by the family, she may choose not to attend or they may prefer to have a separate party for you and the groom at a later time. The same will apply to your mother if your father hosts the party.

If your parents are divorced and regardless of whether one or both are remarried, your mother and father may choose to host the party together, with the stepparents attending as guests.

If your father has remarried and you are close to both your mother and your stepmother, the three of them may choose to host the party. The same rules apply if your mother has remarried and you are close to your father and stepfather.

If both parents are remarried, both couples may want to host the party together. Do not forget that whoever hosts the party–parents, stepparents, or a combination of both–all names should be included on the invitation.

If you do decide to host your own party, you may choose to invite family and friends over for "just a party" and make the very first announcement of your engagement at this time. You may choose to have it announced at the party by your father, who proposes a toast to you, the groom, and your future. Or, if the engagement is a surprise to even the closest family members, you may want to have a large wedding cake in the middle of the buffet table or miniature wedding cakes served individually for dessert as a "subtle" hint as to the reason for the party. It will be a surprise that you and your guests will remember for a long time to come.

If you are one who loves tradition, you will not want to wear your engagement ring until the night of your party or until the announcement has been published in the newspaper. Your engagement ring is usually your fiancé's engagement gift to you. You do not have to give him a gift, but if you choose to do so, the engagement party may be the perfect time to present him with it. It should be something personal and lasting, perhaps a wrist watch that you have had engraved, a leather-bound edition of his favorite book, or a gift that is becoming increasingly popular is a groom's engagement ring.

Your engagement party can be a formal affair, a western barbecue, or a wine and cheese party. If the party is very formal, engraved invitations are issued by the host and hostess for the occasion. If engraved invitations are issued, it is practically a promise that a large formal wedding will follow. If the engagement party is to be less formal, handwritten, purchased invitations, or a telephone call are suitable. Invitations to engagement parties do not necessarily mention the reason for the party. They are generally sent in the name of the bride's parents or of the relative or friend who is announcing the engagement and hosting the party. They are sent to guests who include your family and friends, the wedding party, the groom's parents and their family and friends. Whether or not to invite step families is something you and the groom should consider carefully. Generally invitations are not sent to guests who will not be invited to the wedding.

Guests are not expected to bring presents but they often do. If some do and some do not, you may want to wait and open the gifts at a later time.

However large or small your engagement party is, remember you and your fiancé are the guests of honor. This is a very special occasion that officially makes your intentions public, gives all of those close to you the opportunity to offer their congratulations and best wishes, and allows friends and families to become acquainted. Make certain that, as the guests of honor, you and the groom make all of the necessary introductions. You may be the only two who know everyone–either together or individually–so it is up to you to make certain everyone is introduced. Often, it is best to procure everyone's attention at a specific time early in the evening (or at the beginning of the dinner, if a meal is being served) at which time you and the groom individually introduce everyone. You will want to give their name and their association to either or both you and the groom.

At this time, with the guests assembled and their attention procured (or at the dinner table if a sit-down meal is being served), the father of the bride proposes a toast to his daughter and her fiancé. Everyone, except the bride and groom, raise their glasses and drink. The guests congratulate the couple and then the groom-to-be answers with a toast to the bride and her family and, perhaps, a short speech. When he is finished, other toasts may follow.

Regardless of who is hosting the party, a guest list complete with addresses and telephone numbers will need to be furnished by the bride and the groom. The hostess should give you an approximate number of guests to invite, and the bride and her fiancé should make out the list, keeping within the number. (Traditionally, all of this was done by the bride's mother but times have changed, as they say.)

Make certain you write a heartfelt thank-you note and perhaps even send a small gift of appreciation to the host/hostess. A nice bottle of wine, a bouquet of roses or an invitation to a special Sunday brunch with you and the groom are always nice ideas.

Address Tracking System

The engagement party will be the first of many occasions which will require the names, addresses, and other pertinent information you will need for guest lists, invitations, and thank-you notes. Now is the perfect time to begin a system for keeping the above information filed where it is easily obtainable and current. You will want to develop a system that is easy for you or you may want to use one of the following:

   ❧ Purchase an address book that has a loose-leaf format so that pages can be added as needed.

   ❧ Start a card catalog of your own using recipe cards, alphabetical index cards and a recipe box.

Whichever system you select, make certain the following information is included:

1. Names
   a. Include the husband's, wife's, and children's names, in case you need to refer to them at a later time.
   b. You will want to list whose friend or relative each is, so that if you are unfamiliar with the name.you will know who to contact with any questions.

2. Addresses

a. Make certain to include the entire address with city, state, and zip code.
b. Write down the date you recorded the address. Since you may use this information for years to come, this will help you determine if the address you have listed is current.

3. Telephone Numbers

List both home and office numbers.

4. Guest Lists

Include a space near the person's name (or on the back of or on a separate card in the index) to list which parties he/she was invited to. This will help when deciding on guest lists so that someone is not left out inadvertently or that someone is not exhausted by being included on too many lists. This will also be very valuable when compiling the wedding list so that all of those who were invited to parties will get an invitation to the wedding.

5. Gifts

Note in your filing system what gift was given at which occasion. You will refer to this time and again when writing thank-you notes or when trying to decide what kind of a gift to give this person for another occasion. It is generally always true that people give a gift they would like to receive.

6. Thank-You Notes Sent

Under *gifts*, annotate when a thank-you note was sent. Remember to record the date and the reason for the thank-you. Thank-you notes will be sent to a number of people for a number of circumstances: for gifts given, to friends/ relatives who help, to persons hosting a party or event and so on. Recording dates when thank-you notes were sent leaves less room for error.

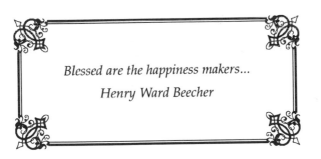

Blessed are the happiness makers...
Henry Ward Beecher

Bridal Showers and Parties

Tradition has it that the first bridal shower took place in Holland when a maiden fell in love with a poor miller. Her father forbade the marriage, denying her the customary bridal dowry. So the miller's friends decided to help the young couple and "showered" the bride with gifts. Today's bridal showers are very different from those steeped in tradition that were given for our mothers and grandmothers. You may be honored at anything from a picnic on the banks of the river to an elegant dinner with wine and romantic music. You may share your dreams with just your girl friends at a quiet afternoon tea or celebrate over cocktails at a '50s party. You and your fiancé may be given a celebration for couples at dawn on the beach or at midnight after the theater.

Guidelines for Showers

❧ These affairs are hosted by friends, and sometimes family, to honor the bride and/or the groom. Although etiquette books say that it is improper for close family members to host a shower, in reality it happens.

❧ Showers should be scheduled no closer than one week prior to the wedding with two weeks before being preferable. Four to six weeks before the ceremony is the most common time frame for most showers to be given, unless there is a shower intended to include out-of-town guests. In this case, the shower should be planned ahead of time so the bride can be free of other responsibilities on the day or two before the wedding.

❧ The bride (and the groom, if it is a couples shower) should provide the host/hostess with a guest list complete with addresses and phone numbers. Except for immediate family and attendants, the same people should not be invited to more than one shower. You might suggest that each shower have a different guest list: for example, one for old school friends, one for co-workers, and one for relatives.

❧ If you know that more than one shower has the same guest's name on the list, let him/her know that one gift is enough.

❧ The hostess's job is to plan the party, selecting a theme suitable for both the honoree and guests. For example, a poolside or garden shower might be a coed party in the hostess's backyard. She may decide upon a champagne brunch or dressy afternoon tea for the bride and her women friends whose gifts are crystal or personal. A cocktail party works well for both genders and all ages.

❧ Decorations are always in keeping with the theme of the shower. For example, centerpieces for a kitchen shower may be teacups filled with fresh berries and baskets filled with fruits and vegetables. Containers for the fruits, too, should be in keeping with the theme. For example, a decorated wheelbarrow is perfect for a garden shower.

❧ An old tradition is to include the words "wishing well" on the shower invitation. This means the guests bring an additional gift of little value but one that will be of great use to you in your new role, such as a box of laundry detergent or a package of sponges. All such gifts contain no name tags and are placed in a replica of a wishing well that the hostess has made. Guests may add an amusing poem or saying to gifts if they choose.

❧ Because of busy time schedules prior to the wedding, shower dates should be double checked with the bride and invitations should be mailed two to three weeks prior to the party.

꙳ When a surprise shower for the bride and/or groom is being planned, the host/hostess should make certain to orchestrate the event so the guest(s) of honor have something planned with the host/hostess or a selected friend. If plans are made without prearranging the bride's/groom's schedule, other plans may have been made that will conflict with the hosts agenda. It would be too bad if the bride could not attend her own party!

꙳ The bride's responsibility is to arrive one half hour early to help with last minute preparations and to assist in greeting and introducing guests to one another.

꙳ Let your hostess know where you have registered so that she may inform your guests if they should ask.

꙳ Have one of your attendants discretely record the name of the giver and the gift received as you open each present.

꙳ You may want to save the ribbons from the packages you open to make a "bouquet" by attaching the ribbons to a paper plate. This is then traditionally used as the stand-in bouquet at the rehearsal.

꙳ Have someone take photographs during each and every shower. The hostess, your mother, or you may wish to make a scrapbook of the event.

⋗ Tradition has it that the groom always appears at the end of the shower. This gives all of the guests an opportunity to meet him and allows him to "fuss" over the bride, her friends, and the gifts.

⋗ Always invite shower guests to the wedding ceremony and reception.

Shower Checklist

Host/Hostess_____

Date_____

Time_____

Place_____

Theme_____

Guest List

_____

_____

_____

_____

_____

_____

Bridal Shower Themes

A bridal shower is a party with a purpose. It is a party where the focus is primarily on the bride. The reason for gathering is to help you get started with new treasures to fill your home, and the guests are primarily your family and friends. It is a party to help celebrate your new future and to create lasting memories that will be forever shared between family and friends.

Mother-Daughter Tea

One of this author's favorite bridal showers is a mother–daughter tea; it seems to be most sentimental and sincere.

The guests invited to this shower include your friends and their mothers (all the ones you grew up with and have stayed close to), your cousins and their mothers, and your attendants and their mothers. The tea, of course, is held in the afternoon, around three; perhaps it can be at the home of one of your mother's friends, a country club, or a historical mansion. Tea, either iced or hot, a blushed wine, bite size tea sandwiches, and an assortment of cookies, cakes and candies can all be served.

At a gathering of this sort, tradition and etiquette dictate that tea and coffee are sometimes passed on trays or served from a specific tea table. A cloth should be used to cover the table with a large tray set at either end of the table, one for the tea, and one for the coffee. On one tray should be the tea pot and all of the accompaniments–the cream pitcher, sugar bowl, thin slices of lemon and tea flavorings. The coffee tray is the same. The cups and saucers are placed within easy reach of the women who are pouring, usually at the left of the tray, because they are held in the left hand while the tea is poured with the right. On either side of the table are stacks of little tea plates, with small napkins matching the tea cloth, folded on each one. Arranged behind these, or in any way that is pleasing, are the plates of food and whatever silver is necessary.

The pouring of the tea is a time honored tradition in several parts of the country and is usually done by two intimate friends of the bride or the hostess. These women are always specially invited beforehand and are chosen because they are close friends who can be counted on for their gracious manners to everyone in all circumstances.

If the occasion is to be more formal you may serve a sit-down luncheon whose menu would appeal to women. Such a menu might include:

Lemon Thyme Chicken Salad
Pinwheel Sandwiches
Traditional Wedding Cookies
Homemade Peach Ice Cream

Fruit and Mint Tea
Tea Kisses

Because the Tea Kisses are such a sweet and unexpected surprise, they are definitely that very special touch you will want to add. The recipe is as follows:

2 egg whites
4 oz. superfine sugar
Grated rind of half lemon, lime or orange

Preheat oven to 250°F. Oil baking tray. Whip the egg whites until stiff. Add the sugar and rind gradually, continuing to beat until the mixture is very stiff. Drop spoonfuls, or pipe different shapes, of the mixture onto the baking tray. Bake for 50 minutes, remove from the tray and cool on a wire rack.

***

At a small tea or a formal sit-down luncheon tea, you invite friends to come at a specified time. For a large, open-house style tea, the invitations might state from three until five p.m. Allow three hours for the tea if the guest list is very large.

To add a very special touch to your mother-daughter tea, the hostess will want to ask each pair of guests to bring a photograph of themselves together, one that they will not mind giving away. The hostess will also want to make certain that lots of pictures are taken of all the daughters, all the mothers, and all the mothers and daughters together at the tea. She will purchase or make a scrapbook ahead of time, devoting a page or more to each mother and daughter invited. During the tea she will have each mother and daughter place their photograph brought from home in the album and write a short note to the bride. After the tea she will add the pictures that were taken during the tea to the ones that were brought by the guests and give the completed scrapbook to you, the bride.

This is a shower given by and for women. The gifts are of a feminine nature, the notes written to the bride are sentimental, and the memories are ones that will last a lifetime. It is a personal time to share your fondest memories and your dreams for the future with your dearest friends, the closest of which is your mother.

⋙ Theme Showers ⋘

Theme showers have become increasingly popular in recent years. These are showers/parties with one overriding element that gives a particular significance and makes gift selection easier for the guests. The theme should be specified on the shower invitation and as much information given about the bride and the theme as possible. For example, the invitation may say: "Kitchen shower for Lori (the bride). Her new kitchen has red trim, is accented with bright yellow sunflowers and she loves country."

Personal Shower

Usually given by the maid-of-honor, this bridal shower can be orchestrated along traditional guidelines or it can take on a contemporary twist and be a great party for couples. The hostess can invite both men and women but have the customary shower gifts be only for the bride. You will be showered with "personal" items that make you feel both feminine and special and some that will make your fiancé feel lucky indeed to be the husband-to-be!

Gifts for a personal shower may include very sexy lingerie; a basket filled with bubble bath, oils and scents; a gift certificate for a facial and a massage; or satin sheets and pillowcases. This author is not too crazy about shower games, however, the one explained below is great for a party such as this and it is guaranteed that everyone will enjoy themselves!

In addition to a shower gift for the bride, the host/hostess has each guest bring one "nice" gift that is a specified nominal cost and one white elephant gift. The hostess will then supply a variety of white elephant gifts, usually one per person, to be added to the pile. The gifts should be for both men and women and should be in keeping with the personal shower theme. Each gift should be wrapped and should have no name tags attached. The hostess will need two sets of dice and a kitchen timer. (One set is enough if fewer than twelve guests are invited.)

When the guests arrive, have these two gifts and the hostess's gifts put in a special place where they will not become confused with the bride's gifts. When ready to play, have all of the guests sit on the floor in a large circle and put all gifts in the center. The hostess will set the timer for a specified amount of time (usually around 25 to 30 minutes) without telling anyone how long, and then hide the timer, usually behind her back.

The rules of the game are as follows:

1. Two people sitting next to each other are selected to begin throwing the dice. They each shake a set of dice, at the same time, each trying to roll doubles. After each has taken his/her turn, one set of dice is passed to the left and one set is passed to the right. The dice go around the circle in both directions passing somewhere along the way. If fewer than twelve people are participating, then one person is selected to begin throwing a single set of dice and the dice go around the circle counterclockwise.

2. When a guest rolls doubles, he/she is allowed to select a gift from the center pile and open it. It must be opened immediately and placed in front of the person who opened it so that all can see it. After the game has progressed for a short while, the person rolling doubles may choose to take another's opened gift, rather than selecting an unopened gift.

3. To allow for more gifts to be opened or taken from another in a shorter period of time (and to double the confusion) the host/hostess may choose to have a wild number on the dice, making it easier to roll doubles. For example, if five is chosen to be wild, whenever someone rolls the number five it is an automatic double with any number on the other die. Doubles can still be rolled in the usual way. If one rolls two wild numbers (two fives), in one roll, then he/she gets to choose two gifts from the center or, from two other people in the circle, or one from each.

4. Each person must wait to roll the dice until the person before them has opened his/her gift and placed it where it can be seen.

5. When the timer goes off, the game is over and each guest gets to keep the gifts in front of him/her.

6. The host/hostess might want to try surprising the other guests with one white elephant gift. For example, she may want to roll up a five dollar bill and stuff it inside the rolls of toilet paper before they are wrapped. During the game no one will want to keep the toilet paper because it is a less than desirable prize. Part way through the game, the host/hostess tells the guests that one of the white elephant gifts has a "surprise" tucked inside. The guests, however, are not allowed to look inside of or unwrap the white elephants until the game is over. This adds an unusual twist to the game because, during the final minutes of the game, the players begin to wonder which white elephant has the "surprise," and they can be seen fighting over something that is worth nothing on the outside but just might have something on the inside!

You will find it most surprising to see which gifts everyone wants and thus get "taken" time and time again. When the players realize that it is about time for the timer to go off and someone else in the circle has the item they really want, the tempo for the rolling of the dice goes wild.

Bathroom/Bedroom/Kitchen Showers

These are traditional bridal shower themes that are designed to help you fill your new home with the items you either cannot afford to buy or, if you are an older bride or this is your second marriage, with items that you may not have purchased yourself for a long time.

For a kitchen shower, here is an activity that everyone involved will enjoy for a long time. The guests retreat to the hostess's kitchen where the guest-of-honor is provided with a bowl, a mixing spoon, and a measuring cup. The hostess then tells you that she will give you whatever you need to make biscuits–everything, that is, but the recipe! As she provides you with the ingredients you request, you proceed to make and bake the biscuits. The hostess has prearranged the arrival of the groom-to-be to coincide with the freshly baked biscuits so he can sample his bride's new culinary talents. The hostess then takes several of the remaining biscuits and freezes them. On your first anniversary, the frozen biscuits are delivered for both you and your husband to enjoy and to help recall the memories of the days before you became an "old married couple," experienced in domestic duties.

Green Thumb Shower

This is a wonderful shower for the bride who loves flowers and gardening.

It can be a typical garden shower with gifts that include gardening tools, seed packets, hand-painted watering cans, decorated or unusually shaped clay pots, plant stands, or books on growing and caring for all types or a specific variety of plants. In the summer, it can be given in a garden or in the park. The menu might include salads with edible flowers and peach-flavored tea whose ice cubes are frozen and filled with rose petals and pansies.

Or this could be strictly a plant shower where everyone gives you a "memory" or "friendship" garden. The hostess might give you a book to record gardening matters. Each plant that is received from your guests can be planted in your new garden. Just as with all shower gifts, a record is kept of who gave which plant. In addition, this list should include what type of a plant it is and, later, exactly where it was planted. If this is recorded, then over the years as friends come to visit, they can walk through the garden which they are so much a part of and you can point specifically to their contribution.

Glass/Lace/Paper Showers

Showers with these kinds of themes make it extremely easy for the guests to buy unusual and treasured gifts.

At a paper shower, the guests should bring gifts only made of paper. This could include books, personalized stationery, prints suitable for framing, and photograph albums filled with pictures of the times that they have shared with you, your family and/or your fiancé.

Here is another "game" that your female guests may enjoy at your all-paper shower. The hostess divides the guests into teams, assigns each team a section of the bride's wedding dress, and supplies each team with a stack of paper napkins, paper tablecloths, toilet paper, scissors, staplers, and tape. From these items, each team is responsible for making its assigned section of the bride's wedding gown. One team makes the train, one the veil, one the bodice, and so on. When all teams have completed their work, they dress you in your new wedding gown and take plenty of pictures for the groom to see. (I personally enjoyed this game more than I ever thought possible. I was so surprised at how creative all of my friends were and at how stunning I looked in their wedding gown!)

Holiday Shower

This is a shower for the bride who loves to decorate for the holidays. It is a time to give you gifts that most new brides simply cannot afford but wish for.

The hostess assigns a different holiday to each guest or requests that each choose her own holiday. She then selects or makes a gift for that holiday. For example, a moss-covered bunny decorated with silk and dried flowers is a wonderful decoration for Easter; quilted Christmas stockings with monograms are perfect for your first Christmas together; a red, white, and blue apron complete with painted barbecue utensils will be used on the Fourth of July; and a papier mâché pumpkin can light up your new house on Halloween night.

An activity that is a favorite for this shower is to have the hostess set up a place that is well stocked with craft items. Each guest then makes

a Christmas ornament for the first Christmas
spent together by the bride and groom.

Here is an ornament that is an easy group
activity. The following items are needed:

3" wide Styrofoam craft ball for
   each ornament
Scraps of several fabrics
Ribbons and trims to match
White glue
Small paring knife
String
Tracing paper
Scissors

1. Select fabrics that will fit
the bride's taste. Using the string, tie it around
the Styrofoam ball to find the exact center. Pull
string ends tightly enough to cut into the
Styrofoam slightly. Remove the string
and, using the paring knife, score the
ball with the knife on the string line.

2. Cut a 6" x 6" piece of fabric for the
back of the ornament. Place the fabric over half
of the ball and, using dull edge of knife, force
fabric ¼" to ⅜" into Styrofoam. Trim excess
fabric close to ball. Occasional use of glue
secures fabric and controls fraying.

3. Plan front half of ornament.
The simplest–and sometimes the most
attractive–is to make both halves alike
with plans to add ribbon and trim to the
score line. Some guests may choose to draw

hearts or stars or trees on the front. Then score that shape on the ball. Place fabric over shape and tuck it into score line. Trim edges. Repeat to fill area between design and back.

4. Cover the score lines with small ribbon and/or trim. Glue ends of trim. Use ribbon or trim to make a hanger.

5. This is most important! Each guest must sign and date their ornament.

Time of Day Shower

Buying the gifts for this shower can be as much fun as receiving them.

On the invitation, the host/hostess assigns a time of day to each guest, who brings a gift that would be used by the bride and groom at that time. For example, 6 a.m. could be matching alarm clocks; 7 a.m. could be a subscription to the morning paper, a bag of gourmet coffee and two matching coffee mugs; 10 p.m. could be raspberry flavored cocoa and flannel pajamas; and 12 a.m. could be a box of turtle brownies or chocolate dipped shortbread fingers and a good movie–for a midnight snack when you just can't sleep!

Another twist to make this shower even more interesting is to add a specific theme to the time of day theme. For example, the shower theme may be personal and a guest's specific time may be 2 a.m., so, the gift might be a cozy afghan, good romance novel, and the makings for a pot of soothing mint flavored tea.

Alphabet Shower

This is another shower which makes the gift buying and receiving a lot more fun.

On the invitation, each guest is given a letter of the alphabet and is asked to bring a gift that starts with that letter. The letters could also spell the groom's name. For example, if a guest is given the letter Z, she might give the bride two tickets for a Saturday afternoon at the zoo, complete with reservations for lunch and zoo T-shirts.

To make this even more interesting, the hostess might want to restrict the theme even further. In that case, she has the guest bring a gift that starts with Z that can be used in the kitchen. The gift might be zebra-striped tea towels with a recipe and ingredients for zoo animal cookies.

A variation on an alphabet shower is to use the groom's name and assign those letters to each guest. Other possibilities are the name of your school or sorority.

Favorite Color Shower

If you love your favorite color as much as most people do, you will adore every gift you receive at this shower.

On the invitations (which are, of course, your favorite color) the theme stated by the hostess is simply that every gift must be this color or combination of colors. For example, if your favorite color is yellow, the gifts could be a bouquet of silk sunflowers in a yellow vase; yellow bath towels or sheets; a yellow basket filled with lemons, squash, and yellow peppers, and a recipe book with a yellow cover.

Invitations for this shower might be handmade. Enlarge the design below onto heavy colored paper and add fingerprint dabs of paint to the edge.

COLOR SHOWER
for
SARAH PALMER

May 14, 7:00 p.m.
at Julie Watkin's home
2820 Polk

Please bring a gift
that is dark green

Gourmet Shower

This shower is especially appropriate for a bride or groom—or both—who enjoys cooking and entertaining. Couples will be delighted to attend this shower, especially when held in a gourmet deli or an unusual or ethnic restaurant that is known for its exceptionally fine food and drink.

Gifts for this shower might include gourmet kitchen items, such as an espresso maker, a coffee grinder, a wok, a fondue pot, or a trendy, '50s-type blender. If the guest's budgets do not allow for such expensive items, they may consider a basket filled with gourmet food items and recipes; a cookbook and the special utensils needed to make one specific entree; matching hand-painted aprons; or a picnic hamper filled with gourmet picnic items such as a bottle of wine and a variety of cheeses.

Here is a game to help all of the invited guests get to know the bride and groom a little better. Before the shower, the hostess should contact both of you separately and ask each of you to answer the following cooking and entertaining related questions, recording your answers.

1. What is your favorite food?
2. What is your least favorite food?
3. What is your favorite type of restaurant?
4. What ethnic food is your favorite?
5. What do you most prefer to put ketchup on?

6. What is it that you wish your intended wouldn't eat in front of you?

7. What is your favorite kind of party?

8. What is your favorite "unusual" or "gourmet" food?

9. How much does a can of marinated artichokes cost?

10. What favorite dish did your mother used to prepare for you?

As you both open each gift, the hostess asks each of you a question that was answered by the other. For example, she will ask you what the groom's favorite food is, and then she will ask the groom what your favorite food is. The guests can see who knows more about the other. It is often surprising how little the two of you will know about each other.

Recipe Shower

This party can be planned a variety of ways. Two options are:

Each guest may give her favorite recipe or cookbook and some of the ingredients or utensils needed to make that recipe.

Or, the hostess may use recipe cards for invitations and enclose a blank one as well. The guests write their recipe on the card, attach a picture of themselves, and write a thought or bit of wisdom to the new bride. At the party, the hostess then compiles all of the recipes in her gift, which is a special book or unusual recipe box, for the bride.

International Grocery/Kitchen Shower

This is a shower that is wonderfully entertaining for both you and your guests.

It is the same as a grocery shower (see page 43) but with an added theme. On each invitation, the guest is given a specific country. For example, Mexico, China, or France. The guest must then bring grocery or kitchen items that are associated with that country. If the guest were given Italy, she could bring the makings for spaghetti or pizza, or, if she has China, she could buy a wok and fill it with sauces and recipes for stir-fry.

For this shower, the hostess may even want to serve a variety of international dishes. She could include miniature tacos, bite size pizzas, egg rolls, and, of course, fancy French pastries.

Herb, Spice, and Sauce Shower

This is a combination between the kitchen and green thumb shower.

For this shower, the guests can bring any gift that is related to herbs and spices in some way. Spices may be purchased from the store in bottles and given in a basket or spice rack, the gift may be the plants and pots to grow your own herb garden, or it may be a book on how to use herbs and spices. Herbs and spices are expensive, and they are usually items a new bride will buy one at a time, so this is something that will make your life in the kitchen easier and more fun.

An added accent to this shower could be to combine the herb/spice shower with an international shower. Each guest must bring herbs/spices from an assigned country or region. The person assigned the "wild, wild West" could bring barbecue sauce or chili powder and sauce, or the guest given Mexico could bring hot chilies and the spices to make salsa.

Tasting Shower

This is another shower that is as much fun for the guests as it is for the bride and groom and is as perfect for couples as it is for just the bride and her friends.

The guests bring gifts that are meant to be "tasted" by the bride and groom when you are settled into your new home. For example, bottles of wine, a variety of cheese and crackers, herb vinegars, marmalades, or gourmet bottled fruits and vegetables are welcome gifts.

The hostess can also give the guests an opportunity to taste a variety of items as well from a refreshment buffet. These can be an assortment of cakes for a "taste of dessert," a collection of fine wines and a variety of cheeses for the "wine tasting party," or an entire array of fruits and vegetables for the naturalist's "taste of nature" buffet.

Grocery Shower

This shower is often the one a new bride appreciates the most. It can fill your kitchen with the basics and some of the extras you will both need and want.

The hostess simply tells the guests that this is to be a grocery shower and then lets their imaginations do the rest. They may bring gifts such as a new spice rack filled with spices; they may fill a fruit basket with canned fruits and bottles of jams and jellies; or they may bring all of the ingredients and utensils needed to make quiche, and package it in a quiche bowl.

For an unusual invitation to any type of food shower you may want to do the following: First copy the following designs onto white paper and type in the desired information. Copy each design on appropriately colored paper, for example, the carrot on orange paper. Cut out each design and place all four designs in one envelope and mail to each guest.

If you carrot all, you will come to a grocery shower for Tina Brady!

HOPE YOU WILL TURNIP ON TUESDAY, SEPTEMBER 10 AT 7 P.M.

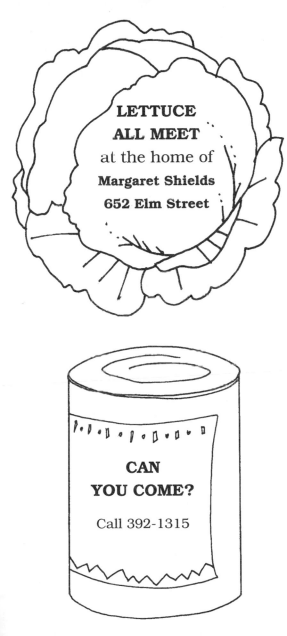

**LETTUCE
ALL MEET**
at the home of
**Margaret Shields
652 Elm Street**

**CAN
YOU COME?**

Call 392-1315

Setu Up a Celebration Shower

This is a shower that any bride will cherish for a long time. Before the shower, the hostess cuts one 12" by 12" square of fabric for each guest and gathers a wide assortment of sewing supplies—scraps of fabric, laces, trims, needles and threads, permanent fine-point markers, and several pair of scissors. She then puts these on a large table in a separate room. Before the gifts are opened, the guests sit at the table, and each makes a quilt square from the materials supplied. When the guest has completed her square, she signs the fabric with her name and a sentiment, if she wishes, and gives it to the hostess. The hostess's gift to you is then to have the squares made into a quilt and presented to you at the reception.

"That's Entertainment" Shower

This is a shower that will give both you and the groom hours of enjoyment when you return home from your honeymoon.

Each guest is asked to bring a gift that is "sheer entertainment"! It could be a video, something just released or a much-loved classic; tickets to a movie, the symphony, or the circus; board games you can play together complete with snacks and cold drinks; or an invitation to a bridge party to be given at the host's/hostess's house when you are home from your honeymoon and settled in.

The packaging for such gifts can be as creative as the gifts themselves. The movie tickets could be tucked into a box of popcorn or the circus tickets could be tied to a bunch of balloons with tiny plastic elephants, tigers, and lions dangling from the strings.

Services Rendered Shower

This is a nice shower for couples who are young and need help to start their new life. It is also a very nice idea, indeed, for the more mature couple whose friends are professionals and have many services to offer.

Rather than bringing gifts, guests offer a service to the bride and groom. In the invitation, the hostess might include a copy of a homemade gift certificate or coupon. An alternative is for the hostess to ask each guest to make his/her own gift certificate from construction paper. On the gift certificate, the service is described, signed, and dated. Then the hostess can compile the gift certificates into a book.

If the guests invited are younger with limited budgets, they can help with the yard work before the wedding, cook a homecoming dinner and have it in the oven when you return from your honeymoon, or offer to help you paint your new kitchen so it is exactly what you want when you move in. If the couples are more established, your friend who owns his/her own bakery can bake desserts for every night of your first week at home; or the friend who owns his/her own landscaping business can offer consulting services free for your new yard, and the friend who is a lawyer can offer to review the legal documents for the purchase of your first new home. You, as the recipient of these services, will want to use them in a fairly short period of time–for everyone's convenience.

"Especially for Him" Shower

Couples are invited and each brings a gift, but the gift is only for the groom. Very seldom is the groom made to feel special by receiving gifts during the preliminary wedding celebrations that are especially for him and this is a nice time to do just that.

An additional "twist" to this couples shower may be to give each of the male guests a gift to open as the groom opens his gift. The hostess should acquire these gifts in the following manner: one week before the shower, she will have each wife (or female date/partner) "steal" something from her partner for the shower that he particularly loves. For example, it might be his television channel changer or a favorite pair of shoes. The wife/girlfriend then delivers the item to the hostess who wraps it up and puts the husband's/date's name on it. As the groom opens his gift from each guest, the hostess gives the appropriate "stolen" gift to the male guest and he is requested to open his gift at the same time or immediately after. It is very entertaining to see the reactions and hear what these men have to say.

Just the Two of You Party

From the moment you announce that you are engaged until weeks after your honeymoon, your schedules will be filled with added responsibilities, details that need to be remembered and attended to, and new relationships with family and friends that need to be cultivated. In the midst of this chaos–regardless of how much you enjoy it–you need to remember each other.

It is important that you take the time on a weekly basis to throw a "party" just for the two of you. It can be an evening together that includes an intimate dinner, a Sunday afternoon that focuses on a ride in the country, or an early morning get-together that gives you both time to relax before another busy day. Whatever it is that you choose, make certain that it is special and that it includes only two invited guests.

What's in a Name?

On a sheet of paper for every party guest, the hostess writes your new last name and gives a copy to each guest. In an allotted period of time each guest must see how many words she can spell from the letters in the groom's last name.

Ask Me Anything!

As you open each of your shower gifts, the hostess will have the giver ask you one question that relates to you and the groom. For example, when and where was your first kiss? What is his favorite color? Where are you going on your honeymoon?

Who Are We?

A modified form of charades played at a shower where couples are attending is as follows: Each couple is given a sheet of paper that has the name of a famous couple with a few clues about who they are and why they were famous. The other couples then guess who they might be. Some famous couples are:

Romeo and Juliet
   Star-crossed lovers
   Tragic play
   Family feud

Rhett Butler and Scarlett O'Hara
   Civil War era
   *Famous quote "Frankly, my dear, I don't
      give a @#&$!"*

Napoleon and Josephine
   French emperor and his wife
   18th century couple

Samson and Delilah
   Biblical couple
   Long hair was his strength

Clark Kent and Lois Lane
   Reporters for the Daily Planet
   Super hero
   Often seen in telephone booths and tights

Roy Rogers and Dale Evans
   Singing cowboy couple
   Famous television western couple
   Horses named Trigger and Buttercup

Donald and Ivana
   Tabloid couple of the late '80s
   Story of riches to rags
   Marla Maples

Li'l Abner and Daisy Mae
Hillbilly cartoon characters
Created by Al Capp

Mickey and Minnie
Famous mouse couple
Disneyland mascots

Robin Hood and Maid Marian
Prince of thieves
Robbed from the rich and gave to the poor
*   in Merry Old England*
Lived in Sherwood Forest

Spencer Tracy and Katherine Hepburn
A Hollywood acting team and lovers
Last movie they starred in together before
*   he died was "Guess Who's Coming to*
*   Dinner?"*

George Burns and Gracie Allen
Television comedians in the '50s
Famous sign-off: "Say goodnight,..."
*   then she repeated*
Seen smoking cigars

Jack and Jill
Nursery rhyme about a thirsty couple
Stumbles and received a severe head injury

Bonnie and Clyde
Infamous gangster couple
Bullet hole covered getaway car
Roaring '20s

A twist to this shower is to assign each guest couple, on the invitation, a famous couple to come dressed as. The other guests must then decide "Who Are We?" and write each one on a piece of paper given to them by the hostess. The couple who names the most couples correctly wins a gift

Pop the Question

At a shower where the couple opens gifts together, the hostess might place questions for the bride and groom inside unfilled balloons. Then she fills the balloons with helium. As the bride and groom open each gift, a balloon is popped, the question is asked, and they must answer it before another gift is opened.

Here Comes the Bride

One twist for a party is to have all of the guests come dressed as the bride-to-be. Each look-alike is judged and a prize is given for the guest who looks most like the bride.

Perfect Match

On the game sheet for each guest, the first column lists the clue below. In the second column, scramble the order of the answers. The goal is to match the answers to the correct clue.

1. What you can do on a clear day in California? *U.C.L.A.*
2. Payment to the court. *Define*
3. What you do with a ladder? *Climate*
4. Workers in an oriental supermarket. *Chinese Checkers*
5. Hot dog in a beer mug. *Frankenstein*
6. Where a camper stays overnight. *Intensity*
7. How a scuba diver catches a fish. *Spirit*
8. Formal neckwear for a hog. *Pig Sty*
9. Where a golfer starts his rounds. *Honesty*
10. What's on the end of a dog? *Detail*
11. What tourists do in Egypt. *Senile*
12. Caused by small shoes. *Agony of Defeat*
13. Proponent of the truth. *Bullfighter*
14. Poor man's transportation. *Wok*
15. Twin boys. *Sunset*
16. A large chorus. *Acquire*
17. Childless couple. *No Kidding*
18. Extra belly buttons. *Naval Reserve*
19. Oriental housekeeper. *Made in Japan*
20. Fortune teller with a smile. *Happy Medium*
21. Unpleasant German. *Sauerkraut*
22. To fluff a pillow. *Shakedown*
23. Inmate's poem. *Converse*
24. Spider. *Webster*

Party and Shower Possibilities

Showers and parties for the bride and/or the bride and groom can be held at any hour of the day and may range from a morning coffee to an after-dinner dessert. The list below will give the hostess several options.

Morning Coffee

Guests should gather around 9 a.m. The menu should consist of either one or a variety of mixed drinks. For example: bloody marys, screwdrivers, or mimosas. You will want to have hot tea, coffee, and hot chocolate available as well. The hostess may choose to have a small selection of plain juices or soft drinks for those guests who might prefer them. If it is to be a buffet, a selection of fruits, breads, sweet rolls, and coffee cakes should be offered. If a sit down breakfast is desired, any combination of breakfast foods can be served.

Brunch

Guests should be invited to arrive around 11 a.m. The menu may consist of similar items to the morning coffee with the addition of several types of salads, vegetables, cooked or cold; a variety of cooked or cold meats, and iced tea or coffee.

Luncheon

Guests usually arrive around 12 and depart around 2:30 p.m. This may also be a sit-down affair or a buffet. The menu should include white wine, perhaps a drink such as a daiquiri, coffee, tea, and soft drinks. The hostess may choose to serve something lighter, such as chicken salad and rolls with dessert or a more substantial course of fish or chicken, vegetable, salad, rolls and dessert. If the hostess wants something served that is a little more unusual, she may choose to serve an ethnic meal selecting from such choices as Mexican, Greek, Italian, French or Chinese cuisine.

Tea

Around the world, an afternoon tea is held in very high esteem and is much more ceremonial than morning showers. It usually begins after 2 p.m. and ends before 5 p.m. The menu always consists of a selection of dainty sandwiches, sweets of all kinds, fresh fruits, mints, nuts, and, of course, tea and coffee. If a more formal menu and a sit-down meal are desired, the hostess will again want to select something such as fish or chicken with the appropriate accompaniments.

Champagne Tea

This always follows the guidelines of the traditional tea with a champagne punch being served in addition to tea and coffee. It offers a more festive air to the traditional tea.

Cocktail Party

This party is held around 6 p.m. or on a Sunday afternoon with a menu consisting of mixed drinks, red and white wine, soft drinks and a buffet of finger foods. You might include a cheese tray, vegetable tray, fruit tray, miniature sandwiches, chicken wings, fresh shrimp, marinated meatballs and other favorite appetizers. It is often best to serve food that can be taken and put on a small plate and does not have to be dipped. A hot cheese dip with tortilla chips or chip dip with assorted chips are not as desirable.

Dinner

These parties usually begin around 7 p.m. and can range from an informal barbecue in the hostess's backyard to a seven course sit-down dinner in a most expensive restaurant. Some type of alcoholic beverage is usually served— beer for the barbecue; cocktails before, wine with, and an after dinner drink are appropriate with the formal dinner party.

Dessert Party

A good time to begin is around 7:30 p.m. with the menu consisting of one special dessert, a buffet with a variety of desserts and a selection of coffees and teas.

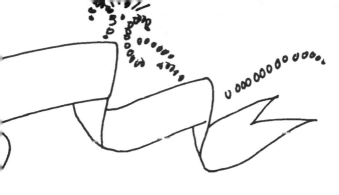

Bridesmaids' Luncheon

"A true friend is the greatest of all blessings" and the bridesmaids' luncheon is the perfect time to say thank you to those friends who have helped and shared so much in the preparation and memories of your wedding day.

Bridesmaids' Luncheon

This party is traditionally given by the bride or her mother but it is becoming more acceptable for the groom's mother, a female relative, or a close friend of the bride or groom to act as hostess.

A large bridesmaids' party includes you, your attendants, the hostess, both mothers, mothers of the flower girl and ring bearer, the flower girl (if she is not too young to come), sisters and sisters-in-law of both you and the groom, and any female relatives or friends you wish to invite. A smaller party would include only you, your attendants, the flower girl, the two mothers and the hostess.

You must furnish the hostess with a list of guests' names, complete with addresses and phone numbers.

Traditionally, the bridesmaids' party was a luncheon that was scheduled the day of the wedding. It is becoming more popular, however, to hold these festivities sometime within one week of the wedding. If any of the attendants are from out of town, the party can be scheduled for the afternoon of their arrival or as a breakfast the morning of the wedding. It may be held at a friend's home, in a club, restaurant, hotel, or tea room. This is a gathering that is intended first and foremost as a thank-you from you to your attendants. It can also act, however, as an opportunity to coordinate issues such as transportation and other last minute details. Sometimes it is the first real chance your attendants, family, and female friends have to socialize together and become better acquainted. It is also a nice break from the hectic pace of the week of the wedding–which is why you should hold it in a place where someone else takes care of all of the preparation and cleanup.

The bridesmaids' luncheon is usually fairly elaborately decorated, often in pink with roses, or in the bride's chosen wedding colors and flowers. A very old and sentimental tradition is the serving of a pink cake in which has been baked one or all of the following:

A dime..................	for riches
A ring.....................	for next to be wed
A wishbone..........	for the luckiest
A heart.................	for romance

Legend says the maid whose slice of cake contains the trinket will be the recipient of the riches it represents.

At the bridesmaids' party, the bride may present her thank-you gifts to her attendants and flower girl, if she is present, or to her mother if she is not. If you are giving special gifts to your wedding party at this time, you may not want to include anyone other than attendants and very close relatives on the gift list. Plan your gift giving to be personal but unobtrusive. Perhaps, you and your mother will arrive early and put out placecards with the gifts at the appropriate table setting. A gift for your mother and the groom's mother may also be presented now. If other family and friends are invited, you may wish to save the gifts until the rehearsal dinner.

Gifts for your attendants should be permanent items of a personal nature that somehow relate to this special day. All bridesmaids should receive the same gift with the maid-of-honor receiving something a little more special. Some ideas are an engraved bracelet, a silver picture frame with the promise of a picture of all of the attendants together to be given after the wedding, an engraved silver pen, or a pair of engraved silver wine goblets.

Some brides today are hosting their bridesmaids' luncheon as an afternoon together "partying" at a health spa or facial salon. This allows everyone involved to be pampered, relaxed, and look her best for the festivities.

After the bridesmaids' party, the guests may wish go to the bride's home to see all of the gifts the couple has received. However, this custom is not as popular as it once was. Today's couples are saving their gifts until they return from their honeymoon and either opening them at a family party or having a private party and opening them together while they are alone.

An alternative approach to the bridesmaids'

party is a "bachelorette" party–one last outing for you as a single woman. If you prefer this type of party, it is usually hosted by your maid-of-honor. You may not feel comfortable inviting your mother or future mother-in-law to this type of party, and it should be held a few days before the wedding. You will have the rehearsal dinner the night before the wedding and you do not want to be so partied out that you cannot enjoy the big day itself.

Bridesmaids' Luncheon Checklist

Hostess_____

Phone_____

Date_____

Location_____

Time_____

Reservations_____

Date Invitations Sent_____

Menu/Beverages_____

_____

_____

_____

Cost_____

Guest List
Names   Gift

_____

_____

_____

_____

_____

_____

_____

_____

_____

_____

_____

_____

_____

_____

_____

_____

_____

_____

_____

Notes

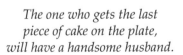

The one who gets the last piece of cake on the plate, will have a handsome husband.

Home Secrets 1898

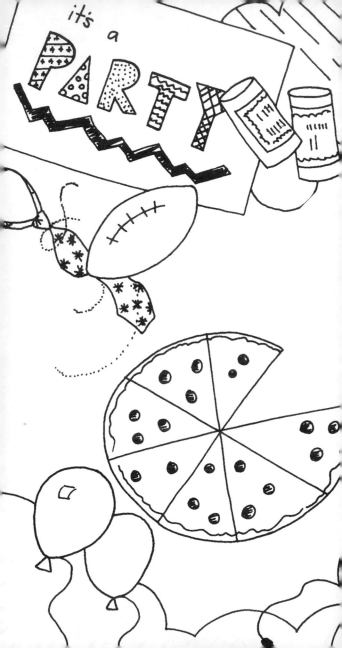

Bachelor Party

The bachelor party is the prewedding party that is most steeped in tradition. Originally the purpose of the bachelor party was to raise a special fund for the groom so that he could continue to drink with his buddies after his new bride took control of the household finances. The tradition then evolved into a celebration whose camaraderie was a way of mourning and saying farewell to the passing of one's bachelor status. Bachelor parties of today are beginning to change tradition once again. They are becoming a gathering or a reunion of old friends whose purpose is to celebrate, reminisce and wish the groom well.

Bachelor Party

Traditionally held the night before the wedding, it is becoming much more accepted to have this night-of-nights the weekend before the wedding. This gives plenty of time to recuperate and allows for the wedding rehearsal to be the night before the wedding.

The party is usually hosted by the best man but can be thrown by relatives, male family members, close friends, or the groom. Generally, all male members of the wedding party are invited, along with other close friends and family. Both fathers may be included on the invitation list, but if they do attend, they will probably stay for a short time only.

The traditional purpose of the bachelor party was for the groom-to-be to celebrate his last night out on the town as a bachelor. Bachelor parties of today which seek to follow tradition often include visits to burlesque shows or casinos, or are held in hotel rooms with strippers and high stakes poker games. Some bachelor parties, however, are more contemporary in scope and are intended to provide close camaraderie with a rousing softball game followed by dinner, or consist of a quiet poker game with catered deli sandwiches for the event. The style and atmosphere of the party will depend a great deal on the personality of the groom. Regardless of whether it is a sedate gathering that includes dinner and a quiet game of poker or a wild celebration, you should not show up under any circumstances. It is a night for the men—you know, one of those guy things!

The bachelor party may be the time the groom chooses to give his gifts to his groomsmen. If, however, the evening's activities are planned to be on the wild side, they might be lost or broken and certainly not fully appreciated. Under these circumstances he will want to synchronize his gift giving with you and choose the rehearsal dinner as a better time. Such gifts should be similar to your attendants' gifts and should be personal and lasting in nature. They could include engraved money clips, hand-tooled leather wallets, monogrammed bathrobes, or fashionable pens.

The bachelor party can be hosted at a friend's house or a popular restaurant or bar. To follow a time honored tradition, everyone toasts the bride, with some going as far as to break the glass, so that it may never be used for a less worthy cause. (The host is responsible for paying for the broken glasses and should notify the management ahead of time, so they know exactly what to expect and do not serve their finest crystal for the event.)

If you are concerned about the traditional activities that are said to occur at some bachelor parties, you should feel free to talk openly with your fiancé about any concerns you may have about the party activities that may have been planned. Make certain that if drinking of alcoholic beverages will be part of the bachelor party, arrangements have been made by the host for safe rides home or for designated drivers.

Today many couples, whose friends are single, are combining the bachelor and bachelorette party into one celebration. It is a perfect time for attendants, groomsmen and other friends to form new friendships of their own.

Bachelor Party Checklist

Host_____

Phone_____

Date_____

Time_____

Location_____

Activities_____

Menu_____

_____

Cost per Plate_____

Total Cost_____

Liquor_____

_____

Cost_____

Toasting Glasses_____

Cost_____

Invitations

Guest List
Name

_____

_____

_____

_____

_____

_____

_____

_____

Transportation Home_____

_____

_____

Total Costs_____

Rehearsal Dinner

Tradition says that a party must be held
on the eve before the wedding and the festivities
must create a commotion loud enough to chase
away the evil spirits. This event was to last
through the night with glasses and plates being
smashed by the guests in the melee. Today's
rehearsal dinner has become a more subdued
affair and is not used as a vehicle to chase away
evil spirits but as a way for the groom's
family to thank the mother and father of
bride for their hospitality and generosity.

Rehearsal Dinner

A dinner or some sort of party almost always follows the wedding rehearsal, which is generally held the evening before the wedding. Even when a small wedding does not require a rehearsal, an intimate dinner on the eve of the ceremony is a friendly way to let members of each family get to know one another.

The groom's parents customarily host the rehearsal dinner. If the groom's parents have divorced, you may wish to select one of the options found on page 9 changing the circumstances to the groom's family. Friends or relatives of the bride, however, or the couple themselves, can also decide to host this event.

Everyone who attends the wedding rehearsal and his/her spouse should be invited to the rehearsal dinner: attendants; clergy; parents and grandparents; parents of children involved in the wedding; out-of-town guests who have arrived as well as other close friends and relatives. It is up to you and the groom to decide for certain whether or not to include dates, spouses, and, if applicable, divorced parents. If all of the extended families are cordial, it is usually customary to invite both parents and stepparents. If the father of the bride is not living with the bride, but is giving the bride away, or is paying for the wedding, then he and his new wife must definitely be included at the rehearsal dinner. If your stepfather is paying for the wedding and/or

74

giving the bride away, then you and the groom must decide whether or not to include your father and his wife.

A rehearsal dinner can range from a formal sit-down dinner with white linen tablecloths to an outdoor barbecue or dessert buffet. A seated dinner that is more understated than the wedding, with simpler food, drink and decor, is still the most popular choice but can be an expensive one. If the hosts are constrained by a small budget, it is better to have a less formal evening and include everyone and their spouses than it is to have a nicer event for just those included in the wedding party.

Invitations for both the rehearsal and the rehearsal dinner should be sent three weeks ahead of time. This guarantees that there will be no questions as to who is invited, when it begins, and how long the evening will last. If the rehearsal dinner is to be formal, engraved invitations should be ordered and issued.

A formal invitation for the rehearsal dinner may read as follows:

Mr. and Mrs. J. Clyde Buehler
request the pleasure of your company
at the Rehearsal Dinner for
Susan Sumner and Ken Buehler
on Saturday, the 11th day of June
at seven o'clock p.m.
Ogden Golf and Country Club
Ogden, Utah

R.S.V.P.
Mrs. J. Clyde Buehler
2800 Fillmore
Ogden, Utah 84403

Response cards should be printed and included with all formal invitations. A response card might read as follows:

Please respond on or before May 25, 1900.

M_____
will attend rehearsal

M_____
will attend rehearsal dinner
Number of persons for dinner_____

An informal rehearsal dinner invitation can be issued on purchased notes with an R.S.V.P. by telephone.

The rehearsal and rehearsal dinner are often the first time your family and friends meet the family and friends of the groom. It is nice to begin by introducing everyone. If you feel it is appropriate, you may want to establish a seating arrangement with place cards for one of two reasons: First, it allows those who know each other to sit together and, secondly, it allows those who are more outgoing to be seated near new family and friends so they may become better acquainted. When filling out place cards, write the guest's name on both sides. This allows unacquainted members aid in remembering everyone's name. You and the groom should be seated at the head table. You sit between the groom (on your left) and the best man (on your right), with the maid-of-honor seated on the left of the groom. Parents and relatives, friends, and other attendants are seated so that men and women alternate. The groom's mother is seated on the right of the bride's father, and the bride's mother is seated on the left of the groom's father. Special seating arrangements will have to be made for divorced parents and spouses and step families. When making such arrangements keep in mind everyone's feelings.

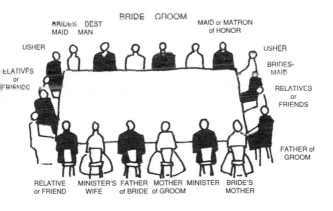

It might be a nice idea during dessert to pass around family photo albums of you and the groom from babyhood or to show a short video prepared especially for the evening. This is also a good time to thank everyone for sharing this time with you and for their help. If you have not done so before, hand out gifts to attendants, groomsmen, other wedding party members, and parents. You can also take this opportunity to go over any last minute details and instructions for the ceremony and reception.

Toasts are historic at the rehearsal dinner. First, there is the customary salute to the couple by the best man (some prefer the host to deliver the first toast with the best man following suit). The groom then follows with a toast to the bride and his new in-laws; then the bride toasts the groom and his family. Attendants might want to toast, also. From there, other guests propose toasts that include anecdotes about the bride and groom. If, however, the toasts go on too long, your fiancé should be prepared with a wrap-up thought to bring the evening to a close and get everyone home early enough to feel rested and relaxed for the wedding itself.

The rehearsal dinner may also double as an occasion to celebrate a reaffirmation of parents' or grandparents' wedding vows, an important anniversary, a birthday, or some other celebrated family event.

The Rehearsal Dinner Checklist

Host/Hostess_____

Phone_____

Rehearsal Dinner Location_____

Contact_____

Address_____

_____

Phone_____

Hours _____

Appointments

Date_____ Time _____

Date_____ Time _____

Number of Guests_____

Number of Tables_____

Menu_____

_____

_____

_____

Cost per Plate_____

Total Cost_____

Invitations Purchased_____

Invitations Mailed_____

Place Cards Ordered_____

Place Cards Filled In_____

Person in Charge of Place Cards_____

Guest List

_____

_____

_____

_____

_____

_____

_____

_____

_____

_____

_____

_____

_____

Rehearsal Dinner Invitations

Stationer_____

Address_____

Phone_____

Hours_____

Invitation Style_____

_____

Paper_____

Color_____

Typestyle_____

Number Ordered_____

Cost_____

Date Ordered_____

Date to Pick up_____

Date Mailed_____

Parties for Out-of-Town Guests

Prewedding gatherings are a traditional, exciting, integral part of the marriage celebration and those who travel the farthest to share in your happiness are included the least. So what better way to say thank you for traveling so far and caring so much than to give your visitors a party or two honoring them?

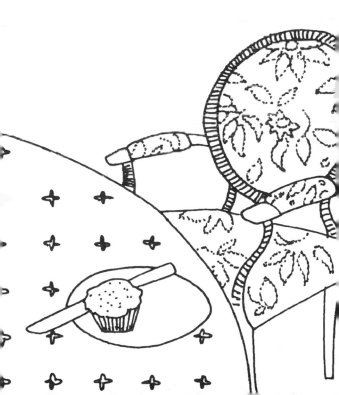

Parties for
Out-of-Town Guests

Welcoming Dinner

If you are having a weekend wedding, your rehearsal dinner may take place earlier in the week, leaving Friday evening clear to greet your arriving guests. This welcoming dinner can be more casual and is usually held in a club or restaurant allowing your guests an informal time to meet the wedding party and the families of the bride and groom. If it is not held at the home of the bride's parents, it allows additional time to enjoy guests they do not see as often. If your out-of-town guests are part of the wedding party, your rehearsal and rehearsal dinner will take place on this Friday evening, the day of their arrival and will double as a welcoming dinner for them as well.

Wedding Breakfast

Friends or relatives of either the bride or groom often host a wedding day breakfast or luncheon for out-of-town guests. Traditionally, this party was a courtesy to the bride's mother, but it has evolved into a tradition that extends a warm welcome and helps make guests' stay more enjoyable and memorable.

This party is usually informal and may or may not include the members of the bridal party. Invitations are issued with a phone call or a handwritten message when guests arrive. You may either join the breakfast or spend the time getting ready or relaxing before the ceremony.

Wedding Breakfast Checklist

Host/Hostess_____ _

Address_____

Phone_____

Date_____

Time_____

Location_____

Directions_____

_____

Guest list

Name_____

Hotel/Address_____

Phone_____

Transportation_____

Will Attend_____

Name_____

Hotel/Address_____

Phone_____

Transportation_____

Will Attend_____

Name_____

Hotel/Address_____

Phone_____

Transportation_____

Will Attend_____

Name_____

Hotel/Address_____

Phone_____

Transportation_____

Will Attend_____

Good-Bye Brunch

This party is held for guests who stay through the weekend after the wedding. It is appropriate on the day they are to depart to hold a brunch to give everyone one last chance to say thank-you and good-bye. The brunch usually begins at 10 a.m. but you will need to check everyone's departure schedules.

Issue invitations verbally or in a handwritten note left in each guest's room. You and the groom are usually responsible for all costs incurred at the good-bye brunch. If the the two of you are just getting started, you will need to decide which family will incur these costs.

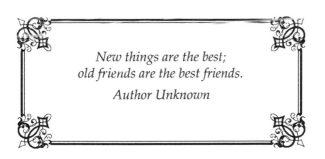

New things are the best;
old friends are the best friends.

Author Unknown

Thank-You Notes

"....Oh Mother—It was so lovely. I wouldn't change one thing..." and so Anne Morrow Lindbergh wrote to say thank-you to her mother while on her honeymoon. A heartfelt sentiment, whether written by the couple to their parents while on their honeymoon or written to family and friends on their return home, is often the best gift of all.

Thank-You Notes

All of the prewedding parties add an air of excitement and anticipation to the wedding celebration. They are indeed a tribute to the two of you and how much you are loved.
It is important that you remember to thank everyone involved for every single occasion. These parties are time consuming, expensive, and acts of love that need to be acknowledged promptly and correctly.

Here are a few basic points to remember when writing thank-you notes:

❧ Send a written thank-you note for every gift you receive even if you have already thanked the giver in person. Be certain to mention the gift in the body of the note and mention what you and/or the two of you plan to do with it. If you are uncertain about what it is or what to do with it, be vague and say something to this effect: "Thank you for the beautifully etched crystal piece. It will be given a place of honor in our new apartment."

❧ Send a written thank-you note and/or small gift to every host/hostess who has given you a party or shower.

❧ Send written thank-you notes to host/ hostess and guests who gave shower gifts within one week of the party.

❧ Send thank-you notes within two weeks of receiving a gift that arrives before the wedding, a month after the honeymoon for gifts received on your wedding day or shortly afterward. It is appropriate for guests to send gifts up to one year following the wedding.

❧ If you are very, very busy, or have an extraordinarily large number of gifts, you can send preprinted cards that state you received the gift and that you will be sending a personal thank-you later. This does not ever replace a handwritten note; it is a courtesy that informs the guests that their gift has arrived safely.

❧ Sign your notes with your maiden name before the wedding, your married name (if you plan to use it) afterward. Never send stationery with your married name on it before the wedding.

❧ The thank-you notes you select may be whatever you like and feel are appropriate for the specific occasion and for the gift that was received. For example, gifts received at a pool side barbecue shower are appropriately answered on either monogrammed notes or printed notes with an outdoor scene. Thank-you notes for formal dinners or, say, a mother-daughter tea should be more formal and possibly engraved.

❧ Make certain you purchase a variety of thank-you notes, or order a supply before hand, so they are readily available when the task needs to be completed. You can save a lot of time by not having to go out and purchase thank-you notes after every event.

❧ Encourage the groom to write his own thank-you notes, especially to his friends and relatives who gave gifts or parties because of their association with him. Customarily, the writer of the note signs it; the other name is mentioned in the body of the letter. (For example: "Sara and I love the crystal vase...") Sign the note the way you and the groom feel most comfortable.

❧ A thank-you note to a married couple may be addressed to the member of the couple you know the best with the other spouse mentioned in the body of the note, or you may address it to them both.

❧ It has become customary to write one thank-you note to a large group (such as co-workers) who gave you a joint gift. It is this author's feeling, however, that individual thank-you notes are more thoughtful and gracious. No matter how much the investment was per person for the gift, each person should be thanked for his/her contribution and thoughtfulness. There are some instances, however, that group thank-you notes are never acceptable, even on a joint gift. For example, bridesmaids should always be thanked individually, as should relatives or friends who are from a distance but have contributed together to give you a nicer gift.

Eight Steps to the Perfect Thank-You Note

1. Address the envelope with the giver's name and address before you write the note.

2. Address the note to the person who gave the gift. Traditionally, you write to the woman if it is a married couple; contemporarily, however, you write to the person you know the best in the couple.

3. In the first sentence say thank-you, mention the name of the person who is not addressed in the opening, and name the gift. For example: "Thank-you so much for the crocheted afghan that you and Mr. Barker sent...." If you do not know what the gift is simply describe it. "...the lovely monogrammed copper piece."

4. Mention something more about the gift, for instance, how much you have wanted one or how perfectly it fits into the decor of your new home. If the gift is money, tell them what you intend to use it for. Mention your husband's name in this sentence, "Because Michael and I will both be attending school this fall, the alarm clock will be a big help in getting us to class on time!"

5. Add one more thought. It may have something to do with the wedding, if the gift arrives before, or something to do with the honeymoon, if the notes are written upon your arrival home.

6. If it is prior to the wedding, sign off with a sincere salutation and your maiden name. Use your married name (if you choose to use it) after the wedding. Sign both first and last names only if you do not know the giver well.

7. Double check to make certain that the correct thank-you note is in the correct envelope and check the name off of your list and be certain to record the date the note was written/sent. You may think you will remember which notes were written, but it can be very difficult. There is just too much happening, and the thank-you notes are too important to make a mistake on the names, to let time lapse too long before they are written and sent, or to let them slip through the cracks altogether.

8. Stamp all of the envelopes at the same time and drop them in the mailbox yourself so you are certain the job is done.

METRIC EQUIVALENCE CHART

MM–Millimeter   CM–Centimeters

INCHES TO MILLIMETERS AND CENTIMETERS

INCHES	MM	CM
¼	6	0.6
½	13	1.3
¾	19	1.9
1	25	2.5
2	51	5.1
3	76	7.6
4	102	10.2

Index

4029